GW00372826

The Greatest in the World ®

by

Vicky Burford

Illustrated by Graham Robson

Public Eye Publications

A Public Eye Publications Book

www.thegreatestintheworld.com

Illustrations:
Graham Robson, 'Drawing the Line'
info@dtline.co.uk

Cover design:
pentacorbig:
book & information graphic design
www.pentacorbig.co.uk

Layout design:
Bloomfield Ltd.

Copy editor:
Bronwyn Robertson
www.theartsva.com

Series creator / editor.
Steve Brookes

First published in 2005 by
Public Eye Publications, PO Box 3182
Stratford-upon-Avon, Warwickshire CV37 7XW

This edition published in 2006 by
Public Eye Publications, PO Box 3182,
Stratford-upon-Avon, Warwickshire CV37 7XW

A CIP catalogue record for this book is available from the British Library
ISBN 1-905151-02-0

Printed and bound by Biddles Ltd., Kings Lynn, Norfolk, PE30 4LS

For David

Contents

A few words from Vicky . . .

If anyone had told me ten years ago, that I would be writing a book on household tips, I would have laughed for weeks! Me, with my constant pile of washing up in the sink and a rather enormous pile of clothes waiting to be cleaned in the corner of the bedroom – not a chance! However, the single life is rather different from running a home with children and so when my first daughter came along nearly nine years ago, shortly followed by my second daughter eighteen months later, I realised the importance of keeping on top of the daily chores. Although I thoroughly enjoyed motherhood – I found myself totally overwhelmed by the constant demands of housework… a woman's work is truly never done!

I therefore set myself the task of finding the quickest and most effective ways of doing the chores to enable me more time for my family (and myself) – and I feel that I have succeeded to such a degree I want to share my tips with you. Male or female, with or without children, life is too short to spend it doing housework, so take a look inside and give yourself more time to enjoy life!

Many of these time, labour and money saving tips have been passed on to me over the years by friends and family (a big thank you to Mum and Mum-in-Law for their seemingly never ending supply of advice) and some I have simply developed myself – usually when in a desperate hurry to clean up before a visitor arrives! I will never look at a baby wipe in the same way again!

I hope you find these tips useful and although I cannot guarantee that they will all work for everyone, they have certainly all come in useful for me at one time or another.

Good luck!

Vicky

The Greatest Household Tips in the World

Ants in the garden

When you are picnicking in the garden, you can easily avoid the scenario of the army of ants crawling up the legs of the garden table to assault your food by standing the table legs in cans or plastic bowls filled with water. Simple but very effective!

Creaking doors and stuck keys

If you have annoying creaking or squeaking door hinges then an ordinary lead pencil is all you need for a quiet life! The 'lead' in the pencil is actually graphite, a brilliant lubricant. First rub it over all the joints in the hinges then work the door backwards and forwards a few times. Repeat the whole process a couple of times and you will soon find that the graphite has effectively solved the noisy problem. As graphite is dry, there will be no infuriating drips on the carpet as can happen when using oil or other lubricants. The effect will also last a lot longer.

This graphite trick also works for sticking or tight newly cut keys. Work the pencil tip over the grooves in the key and inside the key hole as well (do this carefully - you don't want to break off the tip of the pencil in the lock!). Next work the key in and out of the lock a few times, and carefully turn the key until it turns the lock smoothly. If after doing this the key still sticks then abandon it and get another one cut from one that you know works okay.

Chewing gum

Chewing gum stuck to clothing, furniture or carpets can be a nightmare to remove. For clothing and loose covers put the item in the freezer, and wait for the chewing gum to freeze, then you should be able to scrape it off with a knife. Any that remains can be carefully scrubbed off using white vinegar to ease the removal. For chewing gum stuck to carpet, then placing an ice cube on top of it should harden it enough to remove it in the same way.

Efficient ironing

To increase the heat efficiency of your ironing, line your ironing-board, underneath the cover, with aluminium baking foil. The heat from the iron is then reflected back enabling easier removal of stubborn creases.

Mascara

Mascara marks on clothing can be removed with petroleum jelly. Gently rub it on to the stain and let it set for 15 to 30 minutes. Methylated spirit also removes waterproof mascara. After applying to the stain, rinse with soapy water and wash as normal.

Tarnish-free jewellery

To help prevent tarnishing of jewellery place a piece of white chalk or a small sachet of silica gel (often found in the packaging of electrical equipment) into your jewellery box to absorb any moisture in the air.

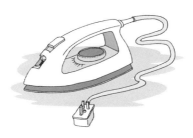

Bathtub rings

Water rings around the bath may seem permanent,
especially if you have spent hours scrubbing at them.
Removing them can actually be quite easy. First cover the
stains with paper towels soaked in white vinegar, leave
them for an hour and then scrub with a little baking soda.
In future, before the build-up gets too bad again, rub any
marks with a wedge of lemon dipped in salt.

Scuffed lino

Scuff marks on linoleum floor caused by rubber-soled
shoes can be simply rubbed away by gently using a large
pencil eraser, or removed by rubbing with a few drops of
baby oil on a ball of cotton wool.

Easy-peel linoleum

To remove a linoleum floor when it is stuck fast with glue,
use a warm iron and a tea towel. Place the towel on
the area to be removed and iron over this just for a few
seconds. This should loosen the glue sufficiently to enable
you to easily pull up the linoleum in one piece rather than
annoying little bits!

Crystal clear windows

There is nothing worse than dull and streaky window panes – and it's always on the sunny days that the smears are most noticeable! It is best to clean your windows on a dull day, to avoid the windows drying too quickly with smears. After you've washed them and before they are dry, polish the glass with crumpled newspaper. Wear sunglasses as you clean, and any smears will be more apparent and if you use horizontal strokes on the outside and vertical strokes on the inside, you can easily identify where the marks are.

To really dazzle your neighbours with sparkling windows, clean them using a cloth and a solution of one part tepid water and one part malt vinegar made up in a spray bottle. After cleaning, dry the windows with a few sheets of value kitchen roll.

Tarnished Silver

Tarnish can make silverware look very drab. Try this amazing way to remove the tarnish and be proud of your silver items. First line the bottom of the kitchen sink with aluminium foil. Next fill with hot water and add about 50ml ($^1/_4$ cup) of table salt, rock salt or baking soda and dissolve by stirring. Put the silver into the sink and leave for two or three minutes. The result is beautifully clean silverware! Miraculously the tarnish is attracted onto the aluminium foil. Finally, wash the silver in warm soapy water, rinse and dry thoroughly. Always have an old toothbrush to hand and use, with a little silver polish, to clean small silver pieces or remove tarnish from crevices.

Tarnished sterling silver can also be cleaned brilliantly using toothpaste and an old soft toothbrush. Dampen the silver and brush the toothpaste on, getting into all the nooks and crannies. Then wash in warm, soapy water and dry thoroughly with a soft cloth. This cleans better than most expensive commercial silver cleaners on the market.

Animal hair

If you keep pets then undoubtedly you will regularly do battle with unsightly animal hairs around the house, on furniture, carpets and clothing. Vacuuming alone may not remove all the hair, but every last bit can be removed easily by wrapping sticky tape around your hand (sticky side outwards) and pressing your hand onto the material covered with hair. Repeating this with fresh tape on bad 'hairy' areas will ensure that even embedded hairs are removed.

Fresh laundry

To keep the laundry smelling fresh, deposit one or two unwrapped bars of soap or tumble dryer fabric sheets between the layers of towels and bedding in the airing cupboard. This is a particularly useful tip when storing clothing that may not be used for a while.

Matching sets of bed linen

To keep your airing cupboard organised, iron and fold all matching bed linen and place inside one of the pillow cases of the set. When you need a new set of sheets etc. they will be together as one!

Non-slip coat hangers

To prevent clothes from slipping off wire or plastic clothes hangers, first wrap rubber bands around the ends of the hangers. If you have to use wire hangers always ensure that there are no protruding metal ends that could snag your clothes.

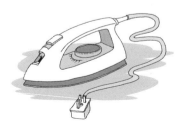

Heat-treated sponges

To disinfect bathroom sponges, wash sponge thoroughly, then microwave it while it is wet, for a short period on high. Watch carefully and, when you see steam from the sponge, the bacteria in the sponge will be dead and you can stop the microwave. Remove the sponge carefully as it will be very hot! When cool, wash the sponge thoroughly before use. Never use this tip with a sponge that has any metal components.

Oil stains on silk

Removing greasy or oily stains from silk can be a nightmare. Try this: first place a clean, absorbent cloth underneath the stain. Next sprinkle baby powder liberally on top of the stain and rub it in with your finger. With another clean, absorbent cloth rub the baby powder off. Miraculously the stain is gone!

Rescuing shrunk woollens

If you accidentally shrink a wool item, wash it in a mixture of hair conditioner and warm water. Gently reshape the garment whilst it is still wet, lay it flat and let it air dry. The garment should regain and retain much of its original size. It's certainly worth a try!

Tight lids

To remove tight bottle tops and jar lids, either try removing the top whilst wearing a pair of rubber gloves or put a wide rubber band around the lid, then twist open. Both these methods work really well.

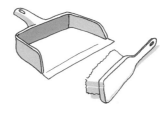

Kitchen bin odours

To help eliminate odours emanating from the kitchen waste bin get into the habit of placing one scented tumble dryer sheet at the bottom of the bin whenever you change the refuse bag. Sometimes a bin bag becomes snagged and kitchen waste can leak out into the bin base. Avoid nasty drips on the kitchen floor by always taking the bin outside to change the bag. Periodically wash out the bin with a weak bleach solution or some lemon scented floor cleaner.

Candle wax

To remove candle wax on carpet or other fabrics, cover the spot with a brown paper bag or a piece of brown paper and run across the top of this with a hot iron. The heat will melt the wax which is then absorbed into the brown paper. Keep moving the bag or paper so you are ironing on a "dry" part until all of the wax has been removed into the paper. You will need to change the paper often to remove large areas of wax. Even old, dried wax should come up immediately and it won't harm your iron.

Grass stains

Grass stains on clothes can be removed by spraying with pure lemon juice and hanging the item in direct sunlight before washing as normal. This will work on both white and coloured clothes and will not discolour the material.

Suitcase smells

To prevent dirty washing from making your suitcase or holdall smell musty on the return journey from holiday, put a couple of scented tumble dryer sheets at the bottom of the case. Before you store the cases away for another year repeat this or use a bar of scented soap in each suitcase for really fresh smelling luggage.

Extension lead storage

To keep short extension leads from getting tangled in storage, insert them into the cardboard centres of empty toilet or kitchen rolls.

Odour-free hands

If you have been preparing fish, onion or garlic dishes and your hands smell to high heaven, then simply rub your hand over a stainless steel bowl, pan or other kitchen gadget – even the stainless steel taps – and the smell should disappear. Alternatively try washing your hands with lemon juice or dampening them and rubbing with salt before rinsing under running water.

Food Storage

Packet foods such as rice, pasta, pulses and cereals etc. should always be stored in airtight containers or jars. Small creatures are attracted to the faintest aromas of these foods and will invariably find their way into packets. Also ensure that any crumbs of food spilt in cupboards are cleared away immediately to avoid attracting bugs. Sweet foods such as sugar, cakes and biscuits are a special attraction to ants, so always keep these in airtight containers as well.

Grubby collars

Dirty rings around the collars of shirts or blouses can be easily removed. Rub shampoo on them as if you were washing your hair, then wash the garment as normal. Shampoo is specifically designed to remove body oils which can be the cause of the grubby collar stains. A cheap bottle of shampoo kept by the washing machine is handy for pre-treating all kinds of oily stains in clothing. Don't forget this trick when you are on holiday!

Wonderful smelling house

To remove unpleasant smells after a party or spicy cooking, boil a pan of water and add some ground cinnamon and an apple. Leave this simmering on the stovetop and you will not believe what a pleasant smell you will have in your home.

Grease stain

A greasy food stain on delicate or non-washable material can be removed by sprinkling the area with talcum powder, leaving for five minutes then brushing off. Any remnants of the mark can be treated with dry cleaning fluid. Alternatively cover the stain with a piece of brown paper and press with a hot iron. The grease will be melted by the iron and soaked up by the paper.

Crayon stains

Baby oil is useful for removing crayon from many hard surfaces. Apply it a little at a time with an absorbent cloth and gently rub until the crayon stain has been removed.

Fresh cake and biscuits

To always ensure that your baked goods stay fresh and last longer put a small piece of bread inside your biscuit jar, cake tin, etc.

Oil and tar stains

A black oil mark or tar on clothing can be removed by dabbing the affected area with cotton wool soaked in eucalyptus oil. To ensure that you don't spread the stain, work from the outside of the stain to the centre and turn or change the cotton wool frequently. Leaving this for about an hour should break down the stain which can then be completely removed by scrubbing the area with soap and water.

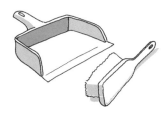

Insect marks

Rubbing a car windscreen with bicarbonate of soda on a damp cloth will easily remove stubborn marks caused by dead insects.

Slippery Shoes

The soles of new shoes can often be a bit smooth and can cause slipping until they have worn in. To prevent this, rub a raw potato over the soles.

Home-made furniture polish

An old but still very worthwhile recipe for homemade furniture polish is to mix together 2 cups of olive oil, 1 cup of water and $1/_2$ tsp of lemon juice. Pour the mixture into a spray bottle and shake well before each use. Use this spray on furniture just once a month and use the same rag when you polish the furniture during the rest of the month.

Quick-drying coat

Here is a great way to speed up the drying of a wet coat. Hang it on a strong coat hanger with a newly-filled hot water bottle suspended inside. Fasten the coat up around the water bottle. The gentle heat inside the coat speeds up the drying process without damaging the material.

Cat tablets

Here is a good method for giving a cat a tablet.
Good luck! . . .

1. Place one hand over the cat's head so that your thumb and index finger are just behind the canine teeth.
2. Tip the head back so that the cats' nose tilts upwards and press gently. The mouth should open.
3. Place the tablet as far back in the throat as possible.
4. Close the cat's mouth and gently rub the throat or blow on its nose to induce swallowing.

Sharper scissors

Here is a quick and easy way of sharpening your own scissors. Fold a piece of fine grade sandpaper or aluminium cooking foil into four and then cut into the folded piece about half a dozen times. Do this regularly and you will always have sharp scissors in the drawer.

Stop cracking glass

Always put a metal spoon into a glass before pouring in any hot liquid. The metal will absorb the heat quickly which will prevent the glass from cracking.

Stronger buttons

To prevent buttons from dropping off garments, put a small drop of clear nail polish onto the thread at the back of the button. When the polish hardens it will be more difficult for the thread to break off.

Sticking zips

To make a zip slide up and down more smoothly, rub a bar of soap over the teeth and work the zip gently up and down until it runs without sticking.

Furniture scratches

A couple of useful tips for small scratches on your polished wooden furniture: first try rubbing the scratches with a freshly-shelled walnut. They should just disappear! Alternatively, carefully colour in the scratch with an eyebrow pencil of a matching colour. The wax in the pencil will also be good for the wood.

Temporary plug

A lump of Blu-Tak makes a perfect emergency bath or sink plug if you have mislaid the proper one!

Plastic bag storage

Every house seems to have a cupboard filled with plastic supermarket bags for re-using. This is a very green thing to do so why not take the time to store them in empty man-size tissue boxes? When you need a bag you can then pull one out of the box just as you would a tissue.

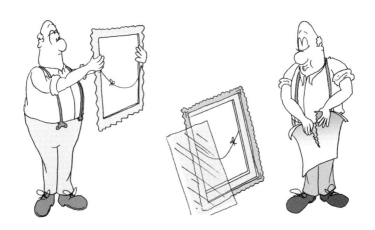

Picture frame

Framing a large picture can be an expensive job. To do this cheaply, have a look around the local charity shops or boot fairs. Here you will often find affordable pictures of the right size and you can just use the frame and discard the picture.

NEWS
Old master lost at Car Boot sale

Spaghetti matches

If you are trying to light candles or a real fire and you have forgotten to buy those useful long matches or tapers then try using a long piece of dried spaghetti. It's long enough to reach most places.

Easy-glide curtain wire

Threading the curtain wire through the top of net curtains can be a tedious process as the end can often get snagged in the curtain material. Cut the corner from a plastic bag and put this or a felt tip pen top over the end of the wire before threading, and it should glide through the curtain top without snagging.

Cleaning artificial plants

To successfully clean and remove the dust from artificial flowers and plants place them in a bag with a handful of salt. Tie the bag and gently shake for a few minutes. This dispenses with the need to ever wash the plants or flowers with water or risk sucking bits off with the vacuum cleaner.

Cotton wool

If you unroll a packet of cotton wool and leave it in a warm place you will find that it will fluff up to about double its original size.

Cleaning Venetian blinds

Venetian blinds slats can be a real nuisance to dust or clean. Try dusting them using a damp 1" paint brush. The dust will get trapped between the bristles of the brush. Be sure to wash the brush after ever two or three slats so you don't end up putting dirt back onto the blind. If the slats are very dirty then put an old woollen or cotton glove or even a sock on each hand. Dip one hand in soapy water and pull the slats of the blind between your fingers. Both sides of the slats will be cleaned but remember to wash the glove or sock out after two or three slats. Use the other hand with the dry glove or sock for drying off the slats. A cup of vinegar added to the soapy water will also freshen the blinds and stop any musty smells appearing later on.

After cleaning your blinds, rub the slats weekly with a tumble dryer fabric softener sheet. This will help eliminate the static electricity that attracts the dust.

Blood stained carpet

Removing blood stains from carpets, furniture or clothes can be tricky but not impossible. If you are quick, the majority of fresh, wet blood can be removed by sprinkling the affected area with cornstarch. This will absorb the blood which can then be carefully brushed off. Reapply the cornstarch as necessary until no liquid blood remains. For any stain that remains, or for dried blood on carpets, first make a paste of bicarbonate of soda (baking soda) and warm water. Smother the whole of the blood stain with the paste and leave it for a while. Soon you will see the blood being drawn out of the carpet into the paste. Then simply clean it away with a cloth and warm water.

Tea and coffee stains

Stained thermos flasks can be cleaned by filling with hot water and adding two denture cleaning tablets. Leave the flask with the stopper off overnight and then rinse well the following morning. The stains will have disappeared. This tip also works well for tea and coffee stains in china cups and is a more delicate way of dealing with your expensive china! If you don't have any denture tablets to hand then try using a teaspoon of washing powder and fill the flask or cups with boiling water. After the water has cooled rinse and clean in the usual way.

Memory jogger

If you have something important to remember the next day, before going to bed put a note inside one of the shoes that you will wear the following morning. Alternatively wear your watch on your other arm as a reminder.

Fresh thermos

If your thermos flask has become smelly then freshen it up by using one tablespoon of vinegar and one level teaspoon of salt. Pour these into the flask, shake well and rinse out thoroughly under running water.

Grubby computers

Because of the static electricity they generate, computers can attract lots of dust and become very dirty. The amount of static they produce can be easily reduced by using a cloth dampened with white vinegar to wipe the keyboard, the exterior of the monitor and all the wires. Vinegar will effectively make the surfaces 'static-proof' and stop the dust from clinging so easily.

Cleaner copper

To achieve gleaming copper make your own cleaning paste by mixing baking soda with a little lemon juice. Use this paste as you would any metal cleaner and finish the job by buffing to a brilliant shine with a soft cloth.

Awkward umbrella

If you find that a collapsible umbrella is not doing just that, then rubbing a candle up and down the shaft a few times should help!

Curtain hooks

When you have taken down your curtains for cleaning, remembering where the hooks went is not always easy. If you make a tiny mark with permanent marker at the position of each hook this will save time trying to decide where the hooks go when you come to re-hang the curtains.

Pure white net curtains

For brilliant white net curtains leave them to soak overnight in a bowl or bucket of water into which you have dissolved a couple of denture cleaning tabloto.

Shower mildew

If your shower cubicle is prone to mildew then keep a spray bottle with a 1:5 part mix of vinegar to water in the bathroom. Get everyone in the house into the habit of giving the shower tiles a quick spray with the solution after each shower. The mildew spores will not be able to survive or grow. By doing this regularly it also makes the soap scum much easier to remove at cleaning time.

Non-crease nets

There is really no need to iron net curtains! After you have washed them spin them dry and immediately hang them back up at the window and allow them to finish drying there. Any creases will simply drop out.

Blunt grater

If your kitchen food grater has become blunt and isn't grating as efficiently as it was, rub the blades with sandpaper to improve its grating ability.

Reduce your ironing load

Don't waste time ironing tea towels, pillow cases, sheets and other bed linen until you actually need to use them. Instead fold the items and store them in neat piles in the airing cupboard after drying. The weight and warmth generated will reduce the number of creases and therefore reduce the eventual ironing time.

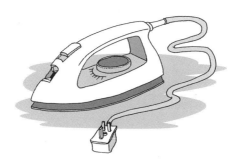

Passport photo

To avoid that washed out appearance so typical of photographs taken in a booth, sit with your head between your legs for a few seconds before having the photo taken. The rush of blood to the head will give you a healthy complexion!

Animal smells

If your pets are making the room smell then baking soda could be the answer. Sprinkle it over the smelly surfaces, let it rest for at least 15 minutes and then vacuum thoroughly. The smell magically disappears!

Scaled taps and kettles

Lime scaling around the mouths of taps can be removed by tying a cloth or wad of kitchen towel soaked in white vinegar around the end of the tap. After an hour the scaling will have dissolved and the area can then be washed with warm water and polished with a duster.

For scaling inside kettles you have three options. Again, use white vinegar diluted with water in the ratio of one part white vinegar to ten parts water. Leave the solution in the kettle overnight. Alternatively, fill the kettle full of water, add two denture cleaning tablets and leave overnight for the lime scale to dissolve. Finally you can dissolve two teaspoons of borax crystals in a full kettle of water and boil for fifteen minutes, topping up with water as necessary. In all these cases make sure that you rinse out the kettle thoroughly and wipe out any remaining loose lime scale in the morning before use.

Mousetrap bait

When laying bait in a mousetrap remember that mice seem to prefer peanut butter, bacon, nuts or chocolate rather than the stereotypical (and probably cartoon driven) cheese!

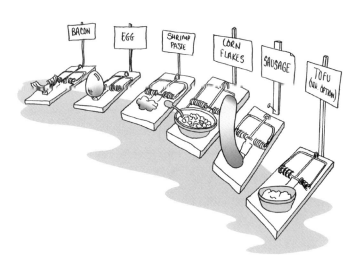

Oil spills

Oil spills in the garage or on the drive should be immediately covered with fresh cat litter. This will quickly and easily soak up the oil. You can then carefully sweep up the litter and apply more if required. Oil or grease stains on a brick driveway can usually be removed by pouring cola over the stain. If this is done in the evening and left overnight, when the cola is washed off in the morning the stain should have disappeared.

Ink stain

The removal of an ink stain on a white shirt can be made easier by rubbing white toothpaste into the stain using a toothbrush or nailbrush. After leaving for a few minutes, the garment should be rinsed and then washed as normal.

Plastic food container stains

Plastic food containers used in the fridge or freezer can sometimes pick up stains from certain foodstuffs. To avoid this happening, spray the inside of the container lightly with vegetable oil before use. To remove existing stains from a plastic food container pack it tight with crumpled newspaper and place in the freezer overnight. The stains should have disappeared by the following morning.

Clogged iron

If the steam system on your iron is clogged then fill the water reservoir with vinegar instead of water. Steaming this through the iron over a sink should quickly clear the blockage. Before use, let two cycles of water steam through the iron to remove traces of the vinegar.

Dry and fresh rubber gloves

After using rubber gloves you should always let them air dry naturally by turning them inside out and hanging them up. Never try to dry them over heat. When they are dry turn them the right way round and sprinkle fragrant talc inside. Next time you come to use them they will slide on easily and will smell fresh.

Heat marked wood

If a hot plate or cup has left a white scorch mark on a wooden table then try putting a blob of mayonnaise on the mark and gently rubbing it in. The mark should disappear!

Vacuum lead

To make the electrical lead of a vacuum cleaner rewind more easily, spray a little furniture polish onto a cloth and pull the lead through the cloth to coat the cable with a thin layer of the polish. It will now rewind much smoother and quicker.

Shower curtain cleaning

The easiest way to clean a shower curtain is to put in the washing machine on a hot wash with a little bleach. It will come out sparkling clean. To prevent the shower curtain from developing mildew, soak it for ½ hour in a strong salt water solution and re-hang. This will stop any mildew forming so remember to do it each time you wash the curtain.

Toilet stains

If your toilet bowl is stained below the water line then pour in a can of cola or drop in two denture cleaning tablets and leave for about an hour. When you flush the toilet the stains will have disappeared.

Water line rings in the toilet bowl can be easily removed using a paste of lemon juice and borax. Rub the paste into the stain and let it set. The stain should then scrub away without difficulty. Alternatively add three cups of vinegar to the toilet bowl, allow to soak for an hour or two then brush and flush.

Stained vases and decanters

To clean the stubborn stains from the bottom of vases or decanters fill with water and drop in two Alka-Seltzer tablets or one denture cleaning tablet and leave overnight. Make sure that you rinse out well before use.

Peg bag

When hanging out washing on a line, use an old shoulder bag to carry the pegs. This leaves both hands free.

Fresh flower water

Water in a flower vase can quickly become stale and cloudy and the glass discoloured. To prevent this from happening and to keep the flowers fresh put a tablespoon of bleach in the water when you initially fill the vase. The water will stay clear for about a week and the flowers will last longer too. Pieces of a potato, cut up small and added to the water seem to work equally well.

Furniture moving

Before trying to drag a heavy piece of furniture across a wooden floor, place socks over the legs of the furniture to help it move more easily and avoid unsightly scratch marks on the floor.

Iron plate cleaner

Scorch marks on an iron sole plate can be removed easily by using an equal mixture of vinegar and salt which has first been heated in a saucepan. Marks on the plate can also be removed by rubbing them with methylated spirit.

Freezer efficiency

A freezer will always run more efficiently when it is full. If you have any spaces in your freezer these should be filled with empty milk containers full of water. In summer plastic pop bottles can be three–quarters filled for this purpose. When you need to make room for food you will have ice-cold drinking water on hand as the ice in the bottles melts.

Cheap hand soap

Often you will find bottles of cheap shampoo at markets. It is always worth buying some to decant into your empty pump-action hand soap containers. It will work just as well but will cost you a lot less.

Fire lighting fluff

Whenever you clean out your tumble dryer outlet be sure to collect the lint and store it in a dry place. It makes a great addition to kindling wood when starting an open fire.

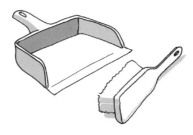

Safer ornaments

If you are fed up with ornaments being knocked off the windowsill by the cat or when dusting, then simply stick them to the windowsill surface using a little Blu-Tack. You will be surprised at how strongly it holds them in place.

Unblocking a Sink

If all your efforts to unblock the kitchen sink have failed,
try crumbling three Alka-Seltzer indigestion tablets into the
plug hole and then pouring down a cup of white vinegar.
If you wait for a few minutes then follow up with hot water,
the sink should be clear.

Spilled egg

Trying to clear up a broken raw egg from the kitchen floor
can be frustrating and messy. Make the job a lot easier
by sprinkling table salt onto the gooey mess. After a few
minutes you will see that the salt has caused the egg white
to coagulate, enabling you to wipe it all straight up.

Easy needle threading

Even with good eyesight, threading a needle can be tricky!
Make the job easy by spraying the end of the cotton with a
fine layer of hairspray and leaving it to dry for a couple of
minutes. The frayed ends of the cotton, which makes the
threading difficult, will now be stuck together.

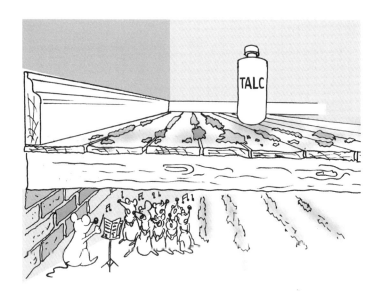

Squeaky boards

To stop floorboards from squeaking sprinkle talcum powder over the offending boards and brush into the joints using a soft brush. Magically, the annoying squeak will disappear!

More airing cupboard space

A few tips for increasing the available space in your airing cupboard . . .

- Fix a pillowcase to the back of the door in which to keep small articles.

- Screw cup hooks around the top of the cupboard to hang up shirts etc... without creasing them.

- Fix towel rails to the back of the door and underneath the shelves on which to hang coat hangers.

Quick drying

If you need to tumble dry an item of clothing quickly after washing then put it in the dryer along with a couple of dry, white bath towels. The towels will absorb any moisture and accelerate the drying process.

If you find you have no clean underwear or socks and they are still wet in the washing machine then use the microwave to dry what is required in an emergency! Use 30 second bursts and check for dryness after each. Make sure there are no metal clips or wires in any of the items, such as under wired bras, or the sparks will fly!

Preventing static

The static found on delicate or light fabrics is caused by over-drying of the material. A wet towel placed in the tumble dryer with these items will take longer to dry than the garments, so the air in the dryer will never get too dry, thus eliminating static.

Cut tumble dryer time

Don't just transfer a bundle of washing straight from the washing machine to the tumble dryer as this will increase the drying time. If you shake each item as you take it out of the washing machine then put it into the dryer, this can speed up drying time by up to ten minutes!

Makeshift eraser

If the eraser on the end of your pencil has gone missing then a temporary one can be made easily by wrapping a rubber band around the end of the pencil until it fits snugly.

Dry felt tips

If you have a felt tip pen that appears to have run out don't throw it away. Dip the tip in vinegar and it will give the pen a new lease of life!

Drying woollens

When line drying woollens you can end up with small stretched sections where the clothes pegs have been. To avoid this thread a pair of tights, a stocking or even a bra through the sleeves of the garment and peg to the line by the ends of the nylon and not the woollen item.

The junk drawer

Every home is almost certain to have an odds and ends drawer where all sorts of small items are kept. It is a good idea to get into the habit of regularly sorting it out and filing these odds and ends into small jars or small bags with a note of exactly what's inside. Fuses, safety pins, picture hooks etc. can then easily be found in an emergency, saving time and frustration!

Longer lasting markers

Marker and highlighter pens will dry out a lot slower if they are stored tip-down so that the tip is always kept moist. Remember to replace the caps as soon as you have finished using these types of pens as they dry out very quickly when the caps are left off.

Distinguishing damp

To determine whether a wet patch on the wall is condensation or damp, attach a piece of aluminium foil over the area and leave for an hour. If the problem is condensation then the foil will get wet on the side facing out – the room simply needs better ventilation. If the foil is wet on the side facing the wall then you know that the wall is damp and it's time to call in an expert.

Ink on leather

Ballpoint pen ink stains on leather furniture can be removed with a little hairspray. Gently dab the stain with a paper towel sprayed with hairspray, and the alcohol in the spray will fade the ink and it will be gradually removed. It is best to try this tip on a hidden part of the leather first to make sure the alcohol in the hairspray is not so strong that it fades the leather colouring as well.

Wooden spoons

Discoloured wooden spoons and spatulas can be cleaned by soaking them overnight in a solution of 1 pint water with 3 tablespoons of lemon juice added.

Easy fold plastic bags

Fold plastic bags over a turned-on TV screen and the static electricity produced will enable them to remain perfectly flat, making them easier to fold so that they take less space and are therefore stored more efficiently.

Fresher ironing

Clothes that have been stored for a long time in the wardrobe can smell a little musty when you come to iron them. Adding a few drops of lemon juice, lavender oil or fabric conditioner to the water reservoir and steaming the clothes as you iron will soon freshen them up – along with the room as well! Adding a few drops of favourite perfume or aftershave to the water reservoir will make clothes smell wonderful for a special night out.

Hem creases

When letting down the hem of trousers or a skirt, the original creases can be removed by first rubbing a bar of soap over the inside of the crease, then using a hot steam iron on the front of the material, protecting with a cloth if necessary. Alternatively, sponge the creases with white vinegar then iron through a damp cloth with the iron on a warm setting.

Iron water drips

When using a steam iron you can sometimes get water drips from the base of the iron which can cause water marks on the fabric. To avoid this, after filling with water wait until the iron has reached the pre-set temperature before ironing.

Discoloured underwear

Over a period of time white underwear can become slightly grey and dull. To help bring the whiteness back, place the underwear in a saucepan of water, along with a few slices of lemon. Bring the water to the boil and keep it bubbling for about ten minutes, whilst stirring with a wooden spoon. Remove the clothes and allow to cool and dry.

Mattress care

You can easily prevent sagging and uneven wear in your mattress by rotating it on a regular basis. Label four pieces of masking tape: Winter, Spring, Summer and Autumn. Place 'Winter' on the top left corner of one side of the mattress and 'Summer' on the bottom right corner of the same side. Now turn the mattress over sideways and place 'Spring' on the top left corner of this side of the mattress and 'Autumn' on the bottom right corner of the same side. Make a note on your calendar to flip your mattress side-to-side and end-to-end at the start of each season and it will last a lot longer! If you find your mattress smells a little musty and needs freshening up, sprinkle with some baking soda, leave for a couple of hours, then vacuum it off.

Avoiding colour-run

When washing multi-coloured clothes, one tablespoon of salt added to the washing powder will help prevent any of the colours from running into the white areas.

Useful carrying bag

When doing a general house tidy-up, it's amazing how many times you'll be in and out of different rooms returning items to their correct place – especially with children leaving their belongings everywhere but in their bedrooms! To save time (and energy), sew up the bottom of an apron to form a large pocket. You can now collect more bits and bobs as you tidy up, and return them to their correct places as you go.

Room fragrance

To make your rooms smell nice, place pot-pourri into the foot end of a pair of stockings or tights, tie it up and lodge it behind the radiator. The heat will release more fragrance from the pot-pourri. You can even use essential oils on the pot-pourri which have aromas to suit the particular room, e.g. lavender in the bedroom, rose in the lounge, vanilla or apple in the kitchen, lemon in the bathroom.

Another way to quickly freshen up a room is to drop a small dot of perfume on the bulb of your table-lamps and the heat will disperse your favourite fragrance into the room.

Dryer sheet replacements

Scented tumble dryer sheets can work out expensive – especially if you have a large household! The alternative is to make your own scented sponges which do the job just as well as the bought sheets and are a much more cost-effective option. Take a cheap bath sponge, cut it up into squares and drop these in a container of your favourite, liquid, fabric softener. Keep this near the tumble dryer. When you are placing clothes in the dryer simply take one of the sponge pieces from the container, squeeze it out completely and add this to the clothes. At the end of the cycle they will smell wonderful! This also helps to reduce annoying static in the garments.

Foggy screen

A misted car windscreen can be cleaned more efficiently by using a chalkboard eraser rather than a cloth.

Broken glass

To clear up small splinters or shards of broken glass, use a thick slice of bread and press gently over the area. Alternatively you can use several folded sheets of slightly dampened kitchen paper. Although both these methods are effective for picking up minute pieces of broken glass, larger pieces should first be removed by hand, taking care to avoid any injuries.

Bath rings

To rid your bath of unsightly rings of grime, fill the bath with warm water, adding two cups of biological washing power under the running tap. Leave to soak overnight and rinse away in the morning to reveal a lovely clean bath! Alternatively use cold water and add ½ pint of bleach for the same effect. Ensure that you wash the bath down thoroughly before use.

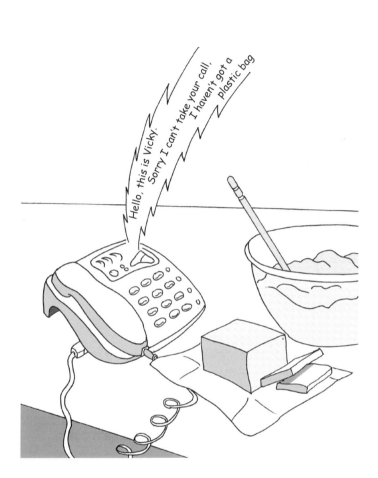

Floury hands

You can virtually guarantee that the phone will ring when you are baking and as soon as your hands are covered in grease and flour! Before you start preparing to cook, always keep a plastic bag nearby to pop on quickly and avoid either a very messy phone, or a missed call.

Ants

If you are troubled with ants, find their way in and pour a line of flour to block their route or around the edge of cupboards or shelves that they are attracted to, as ants will not cross a line of flour. The same also applies to chalk, so if you have any to hand, draw chalk lines in your cupboard as a barrier. Ants are also put off by the smell of mint, so place some fresh sprigs in any areas the ants appear.

Tomato ketchup stain

To remove a tomato ketchup stain (or in fact any pickle or sauce stain) from material you must act quickly. For washable fabrics, first remove as much of the excess as possible then rinse under running cold water, from the reverse of the material if feasible, to force the stain out. Then sponge the area with warm water and washing-up liquid or upholstery shampoo if you are dealing with furniture fabric or a carpet. If stain remains, as can happen with strong sauces, then dab the area carefully with methylated spirits. Finally, wash the garment as normal. For non-washable items, again remove as much of the excess sauce as possible but gently sponge with just cold water then blot with tissues or a clean dry cloth. If the stain persists then a visit to the dry cleaners is called for!

Lost contacts

If you drop a contact lens then don't panic! It's easy to find if you darken the room and shine a torch around. The lost contact lens will reflect the light from the torch so watch carefully as you move the beam systematically across the floor. Remember that a contact lens can land on and stick to a vertical surface too!

Scuffed shoes

If you don't have any of the correct polish then an easy way to touch up scuff marks on shoes is to use a permanent felt tip pen of the same colour as the shoe.

Refrigerator odours

To eliminate unpleasant or overpowering odours in the refrigerator place a small bowl of baking soda in the fridge to help absorb the smells. Keeping a piece of charcoal in your refrigerator will also absorb any strong odours and keeps the interior smelling sweet. Remember to replace the piece of charcoal every 5 – 6 months or sooner if you have had very strong smelling foods in the refrigerator. A wad of cotton wool soaked in vanilla essence will also keep the inside smelling fresh.

Masking cooking smells

To remove the lingering smells after you have cooked and eaten a meal, heat some fresh orange or lemon peel in the oven (gas mark 4/350˚F/180˚C) for 10 to 15 minutes. Your kitchen aroma will then be replaced with a fresh citrus scent. A few vanilla pods left in an open jar in the kitchen will also help.

Chopping board

If your chopping board smells because you have been cutting foods such as onions, garlic or fish, rub the board thoroughly with half a cut lemon. The acid in the lemon will neutralise the strong odours lingering on the wood.

Carpets

To give your carpets a really thorough clean, before vacuuming first use a stiff bristled house-broom and sweep the carpet against the pile. This will help to dislodge the dust and dirt. After sweeping, vacuum thoroughly and your carpets will look clean and rejuvenated.

Milk pans

You will find that milk saucepans are much easier to clean if, immediately after use, they are turned upside down and left to stand for a few minutes before washing.

Towel storage

A wooden wine rack makes an attractive storage solution for clean towels in the bathroom. The towels can be rolled and placed in the wine bottle compartments.

Sticking drawers

Drawers that feel stiff to open can be so aggravating! Rubbing candle wax along the runners should make them open much more smoothly.

Candle wax on wood

Candle wax stains on a wooden surface can be removed effectively in the following way: with a hairdryer, gently melt the wax enough to allow you to wipe it away with an absorbent cloth. Then remove any residue from the wood using a 1:10 part vinegar and water solution.

Tea spills

When you are pouring tea, if it spills or drips on to the tablecloth immediately sprinkle sugar on the spill. Wash the tablecloth in the usual way and the tea stain will disappear.

keep flowers and fruit apart

If you have ever wondered why your vases of beautiful cut flowers don't last more than a few days, take a look around the room. If you have a bowl of fruit anywhere – that is the reason. The gas (ethylene), which fruits give off as they ripen, will fade cut flowers very quickly. The further the distance the fruit is away from the flowers the longer the blooms will last!

Dusty doormat

A dusty doormat can be cleaned without creating clouds of dust by placing it in a large dustbin liner before shaking it vigorously.

Salt

Because of salt's naturally abrasive quality, it is ideal for removing burn marks from dishes and stains on crockery. Black marks on cutlery, caused by eggs for instance, can also be removed when salt is used on a cloth to rub the marks gently away.

Burnt pans

To remove burn marks from pans or oven trays, sprinkle the areas with baking soda and moisten slightly with water. Leave to stand overnight then rinse thoroughly in warm water. Most of the burnt bits will wash away, but a wooden spoon or spatula may be required to remove very stubborn marks. Covering burnt food in the bottom of a pan with cola and simmering for 10 minutes can also make the residue easier to scrape off.

Fat spills

If you spill hot fat either on the kitchen work surface, or on the floor, then pour cold water gently over the fat immediately. This will help it solidify, making it much easier to clean up. Afterwards wash the area with hot soapy water.

Oven doors

As part of your general cleaning routine, you can wipe your oven door or hob with white wine vinegar. Not only does it cut through grease and grime well, but it will also leave the surface nice and shiny.

Fresh kitchen

If you are going away for a few days a simple way of ensuring that you return to a fresh smelling kitchen is to leave out a cut lemon in a dish.

Comfortable ironing

Ironing can be a long and tiring business so learn to sit down when ironing. If you prefer to stand, then remove your shoes and stand on a large soft cushion. This will ease your feet and prevent tiredness.

Bathroom cleaning

Before you clean your bathroom, close the door and run some hot water into the bath to build up some steam. This will make the cleaning process quicker and easier as the grime and mildew is loosened in the warm, damp conditions.

Soap dish

A quick trick to stop the soap from sticking is to rub a little petroleum jelly on to your soap dish.

Spare bed freshness

If you are going away on holiday or if you have a spare bed that is not used regularly then leave a fabric conditioner sheet between the sheets to ensure a welcoming and fresh smell when the bed is next slept in. It is also advisable to air a little-used bed for a couple of hours before its next use.

Ironing sleeves

To iron a jacket without a crease along the sleeve, roll up a
thick magazine, cover with cloth and push into the sleeve.
The magazine will immediately unroll, making a firm pad
which will allow you to iron the sleeve without creating a
creased edge.

Damp dusting

Moistening a dusting cloth very slightly with water before use will ensure a more efficient job as dust will adhere to the damp cloth, rather than just float off into the room.

Handy toothbrushes

Keep an assortment of old toothbrushes, soft and firm bristles, as they make ideal cleaning tools either for the gentler jobs, like cleaning jewellery, or the more abrasive requirements like scrubbing away mould in the bathroom. They are also useful for cleaning the inaccessible crevices in wire whisks, graters, garlic presses etc.

Woodlice

Woodlice are always attracted to damp areas in the home so sprinkling a little talcum powder over these areas will help to deter them. If it is an area where food may be stored and you want to avoid the aroma of talc tainting the food, then use baking powder instead which will have the same effect.

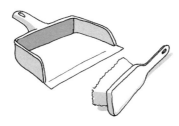

Dried flowers and herbs

Using the microwave is a quick and easy method for drying flowers or herbs. Place a single layer of the herbs or flowers between two pieces of paper kitchen towel and microwave for two minutes. Leave to stand for a minute then repeat the process, microwaving for 20 seconds at a time, until the plants are dry. Because of their size, flowers will take a little longer to dry than herbs.

Old net curtains

If you have an old net curtain, cut and sew up sections of it to make useful laundry bags for your washing and drying. Delicate clothes can be washed separately in a bag, to prevent them from getting snagged by zips etc. on other garments, and socks and underwear can be separated into different bags to avoid them getting mixed up in the wash. This is especially useful for families with young children, as it saves valuable time spent sorting socks!

Mice deterrents

To prevent mice from getting into your garden shed or garage, block up any openings with balls of steel wool. Mice will not chew through these. Sprinkling ground cayenne pepper or peppermint oil around the perimeter of the building and near any possible entry holes will also help as mice hate these smells.

Hard water

Coloured clothes can, over a period of time, become dulled if you have hard water. A quick and easy remedy is to add a teaspoon of salt to your washing powder. Amazingly the colour of the clothes will be rejuvenated.

Frost-free washing

If you have a washing load to line-dry and you are worried about the temperature dropping low and the whole lot freezing solid then fear not! A little table salt added to the final rinse will ensure that the clothes will not end up like pieces of board on the line as it prevents the water in the damp garments from freezing.

Plate warming

To heat plates for a large number of dinner guests when you have a full oven, put them in the microwave for a few minutes or in the dishwasher on a short or drying cycle. The plates that is, not the guests!

Smelly trainers

The problem of smelly trainers or tennis shoes can be dealt with in a couple of ways. A good sprinkling of baking soda into each shoe will absorb the smell overnight, with the baking soda being vacuumed out of the shoes in the morning. For the same effect, stuff the shoes overnight with the foot ends of tights or stockings filled with cat litter.

Kitchen roll holder

For that tidy 'Al Fresco' dining experience put your patio table umbrella through the centre of a kitchen roll before putting the pole through the table. The kitchen roll will be easily available to everyone and won't roll or blow away.

Instant improvement

If you are short of time and can't do a complete clean of a particular room then just do a quick tidy. Put everything away in its right place, clear up any used crockery, throw away any fading or dead flowers and empty the waste bin. Finally give a quick spray of air freshener. The room will instantly look much better!

Copper pans

If you have copper-bottomed pans that are looking dull or discoloured, smear tomato sauce over the copper and leave to stand for a couple of hours. Rinse and wash in the usual way and the copper will be rejuvenated and shiny.

Start at the top

When tackling the job of cleaning the whole house in one go remember to start at the top and work down. By doing this you are working with gravity with any dislodged dust making its way down to lower levels. Also, for every room, always vacuum or sweep it first as this generally raises dust.

As you work your way around the house on a cleaning mission, take a plastic rubbish bag with you. When emptying waste paper bins this will save you have to go to and from the main rubbish bin.

Crystal clear decanter

Drying the inside of a crystal decanter or narrow neck vase can be difficult and water marks can often develop if left to dry naturally. An easy way to dry the decanter or vase quickly without marks is to hold the bottom of the vessel under running hot water with the opening held away from the water. The heat will cause any water inside to evaporate leaving it perfectly dry and mark free.

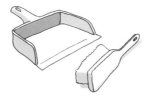

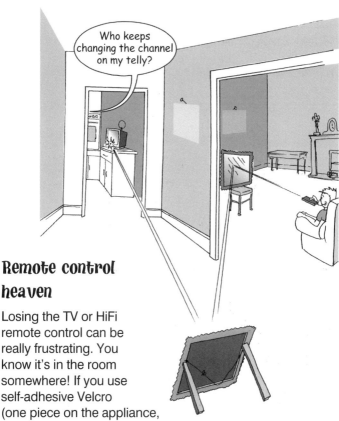

Remote control heaven

Losing the TV or HiFi remote control can be really frustrating. You know it's in the room somewhere! If you use self-adhesive Velcro (one piece on the appliance, one piece on the remote) you can then attach the remote to the side of the TV or HiFi after use.

Here's one for the real couch potatoes! If you have to keep getting out of your seat because, from where you are sitting, the infra red from the remote control is not in view of the sensor on the equipment, then simply position a mirror opposite the set and direct the remote to the mirror. The signal beam will then bounce off the mirror to the sensor!

Toilet lime scale

A good way to remove lime scale from the toilet is to drop in two denture cleaning tablets and leave overnight, without flushing. The next morning the toilet pan should be completely clean.

Nettle repellent

A bunch of stinging nettles grown in front of an open window or door will discourage flies and wasps from entering the house. The nettles will also attract some colourful butterflies. Take care, however, if there are young children around

Longer-lasting nylons

Stretching new tights or stockings before wearing them will make them last longer. You can also prevent fine nylons from laddering by spraying them lightly with hairspray. Another good tip to extend the life of nylons is to wash the new pair in warm water, squeeze dry in a towel, place in plastic bag and put in them in the freezer overnight. Thaw them the next day and hang them out to dry before wearing.

Coffee jar castor cups

If you are worried about the feet or castors of furniture marking wooden floors or denting carpets then save the plastic lids from coffee jars and use these as protective castor cups. You may find that you have to change your brand of coffee to get a lid that matches your furniture or carpet!

Beetroot staining

Beetroot stains can be more effectively removed from clothes if you rub the cut face of a pear over the stain first.

Scrambled egg

After preparing scrambled egg, make cleaning the saucepan easier by holding it upside down under cold running water for a few minutes immediately after use.

Barbeque grill

Rub the grill of a barbeque with a cut, raw potato before each use to help keep it clean; after use, washing away burnt food and fat will be a much easier job. To clean a barbeque grill that is already badly encrusted soak it in leftover brewed filter coffee overnight, then scrub well and wash as normal. Another good way of loosening any burnt on grease is to lay the barbeque grill on the lawn overnight. The dew will combine with the enzymes in the grass and make the cleaning job a whole lot easier. This also works well with dirty wire oven racks.

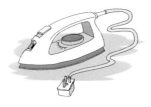

Oven doors

The worse of the burnt-on food stains on a glass oven door can be removed with a disposable razor before cleaning as normal.

Leaky washing machine

A bicycle puncture repair kit can be used to patch small holes in a leaking rubber door seal of an automatic washing machine. If you can't repair it immediately then turn the seal round so that the worn or punctured part is at the top, but don't leave it too long to fix.

Gleaming sink

The stainless steel surface of a sink can be made to really gleam by sprinkling the dry sink surface with a little flour then buffing up with a soft cloth.

Carpet indentations

It can be really annoying when you rearrange the furniture only to find indentations in the carpet. There are, however, a couple of neat tricks to remove them. First try putting an ice cube on the dented carpet pile and allow it to slowly melt. As it does the water will seep into the fibres and cause them to rise up again. Alternatively hold a steaming iron just above the dented carpet and force the steam into the carpet pile using the 'extra steam' button on the iron. Be careful not to allow the iron to touch the carpet. The fibres should spring back into place. Finally, with either of these methods, use a stiff brush to lift up the fibres.

Moving kitchen appliances

If you have to move large kitchen appliances such as refrigerators or cookers to clean behind them then sprinkle some talcum powder on the floor in front of them and they should slide out a lot easier.

Insects

To help keep your home free from troublesome insects, make up a solution of water and tea tree oil and spray this around the doors and windows where the insects could gain entry. This should keep them away. Cotton wool balls dampened with lavender essence oil will also discourage flies from the house.

Frozen water bottles

An alternative to freezer blocks for a cool box on a picnic is to freeze small bottles of water. These will not only keep the food chilled but also provide ice cold drinks as the ice in the bottles melts.

Wake up call

If you are one of those people who really has trouble waking up in the morning, despite the alarm going off, then maybe your brain has become accustomed to this noise that frankly you would rather not hear! Try plugging the bedside light, radio, TV etc. into a trailing socket plugged into an electronic timer so that everything comes on at once. Annoying maybe, but it's a sure way of not missing an important appointment!

Easier defrosting

After defrosting your freezer, dry the inside well and then apply a thin layer of glycerine to all the internal surfaces. When you next defrost the freezer the ice will come away much easier.

Stuck glasses

Two glasses that are stuck together – one inside the other – can be easily separated without any damage. Stand the bottom glass in hand hot water and fill the top glass with cold water. The two should then easily come apart!

Easy clean oven

After cleaning your oven, rub the inside with a water and bicarbonate of soda paste. This will make the oven much easier to clean next time.

Rust spots

All traces of rust on kitchen utensils can be easily removed using a wine cork dipped in olive oil.

Fluff on clothes

When washing dark coloured clothes prevent them from picking up fluff by turning them inside out first.

Misty watch

If the glass face of your wristwatch gets misted up then simply turn the watch over and wear it with the glass next to your skin for a while. The mist should then clear.

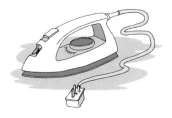

Vacuum cleaner filter

When vacuuming in the deep crevices down the back of chairs and sofas put a sock or stocking over the end of the vacuum cleaner nozzle. This will ensure that any loose change, earrings and other small items are not sucked into the cleaner.

Shopping list

It is a very good idea to keep a copy of every shopping list you make and be sure to add those items you remember in the supermarket. After a few months you can spend a little time rewriting these lists into one comprehensive list to which you can refer every time you need to make a new list.

Cooking spills

Whenever you are cooking, keep to hand a dishcloth dampened with clean soapy washing-up water. This enables you to mop up any cooking spills immediately before they become cooked or dried on and difficult to remove.

Picnic condiments

Used herb and spice jars make very useful containers for salad dressings and other condiments when going on a picnic or for 'al fresco' dining, when you would rather not have the bigger bottles on display.

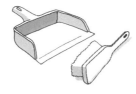

Saving on liquid soap

Pump action liquid soap containers are very useful but children do have a habit of using far too much. Solve this by putting a rubber band around the base of the pump so that the plunger cannot go down as far. This will allow them to still "pump out" plenty of the soap to clean their grubby hands, but they will not use as much and will create less mess! You will probably find that the reduced amount of delivered soap is still plenty for your hands too. Do the manufacturers deliberately make the bottle deliver more than we need in one squirt? Surely not!

Dry jars

After washing and drying twist-top jam jars put crumpled kitchen paper inside before storing. This will absorb any remaining moisture and prevent the lids from corroding.

Rust rings

Cans such as hairspray or shaving foam, can leave a rusty and unsightly mark on shelves, especially in a damp bathroom. To prevent this happening, apply a thin coat of clear nail varnish to the bottom of the can, making sure it's dry before standing on the shelf. Water will no longer be able to penetrate the metal, so rusting will not occur.

Non-crack glassware

If you rub the outside of a glass or earthenware casserole dish with a raw onion before cooking, then this will prevent the dish from cracking as it is heated.

Bacteria-free kitchen

Baby's bottle sterilising fluid is a great anti-bacterial cleaner for around the kitchen - work surfaces, chopping boards, bread boards, mugs, teapots and dishes.
After use the same solution can be used to freshen up dishcloths, sponges, vegetable brushes etc. and then, finally, poured down drains to keep them smelling fresh.

Damp towels

Get your family out of the habit of hanging their damp towels over the wooden banister, which will cause the paint or varnish to wear more quickly. Instead, if there is a shortage of bathroom space, persuade them to hang the towels in the airing cupboard or from a hook on the back of their bedroom door.

Brighter floor

A kitchen floor can look dull after mopping. To brighten the floor, wipe it over with a solution consisting of one cup of white vinegar in a bucket of water.

Home-made hiding place

Finding a good, safe storage place for money and small valuables in the house can be difficult. A good trick is to spray the inside of an empty, clean mayonnaise jar with white paint. Leave the label on the jar and simply drop your precious items into the jar and store in the refrigerator. Let's hope not too many burglars buy this book!

Refrigerator mildew

Mildew inside a refrigerator can be prevented by occasionally wiping down the insides with white vinegar.

Potato peeler

When a potato peeler becomes blunt it can be sharpened using an old nail file inserted into the slot in the peeler and rubbed along the edge of the cutter.

Kitchen blender

An easy way to clean a food blender after use is to fill the container halfway with hot water and add a couple of drops of dishwasher detergent or half a teaspoon of dishwasher powder. Cover the blender, turn on for a few minutes, rinse and dry.

Endless sticky tape

If you always seem to spend more time trying to find the end of a roll of sticky tape than actually using it, try sticking a small button on the end of the tape when you have finished with it. Next time you come to use the tape you can just move the button along and that stressful time with your fingernail will be a distant memory!

Treating stains

When working on any stain always move from the outside to the middle of the stain when attempting removal. Starting at the centre and moving outwards will just succeed in spreading the problem.

Bathroom tiles

Off coloured white grout between bathroom tiles can be restored by using canvas shoe whitening cream. Run the sponge applicator down the lines of grouting, leave for a few minutes then wipe away any excess from the surface of the tiles.

Lost toothpaste cap

If the top of a tube of toothpaste goes missing then the paste can very quickly dry hard and it becomes unusable. If this happens, simply store the tube upside down in a glass of water, changing the water daily to prevent it from becoming stale.

Blocked nozzle

To unblock the nozzle of an aerosol can, remove it and place it in a saucepan of boiling water for a few seconds. This should melt and remove the blockage. Leave the nozzle to dry before replacing it on the can.

Soapy sponge

A great ready-soaped sponge can be made by cutting a slit into the side of a large bath sponge and slipping in any leftover pieces of soap. This is a good way of recycling those bits of soap you would normally throw away and also ensures the kids always use soap in the bath!

Clogged hairbrush

If a hairbrush becomes clogged with hair then soak it for half an hour in a solution of warm water and conditioning shampoo. All the hair should then easily come off the brush. It is a good idea to do this regularly to ensure that hairbrushes are always clean.

Sticking rubber gloves

Surprisingly, rubber gloves can be more difficult to remove
if you have been using them in hot water as your hands
tend to get a bit sweaty and swell slightly. To easily remove
the gloves, first run cold water over them.

Waterproof umbrella

Umbrellas are water repellent to a certain degree but rarely waterproof, as a heavy rainstorm will often reveal! A dry umbrella can be made virtually water resistant by spraying both sides with hairspray and drying completely before folding away. A good tip for drying a wet umbrella is to leave it half open so that the material doesn't stretch and become detached from the spokes.

Travelling with confidence

It is a really good idea to photocopy all of your important travel documents – passport, insurance, itinerary etc… - before you go abroad and pack them separately from the originals. If any of your documents are lost you will still have all the information you require. When you return from your holiday make a list of all those items that you took and did not use along with a note of those things that you wish you had taken. Put the list in your suitcase ready to make your packing more efficient next time you travel.

Potato peel kindling

If you have an open fire you will know the benefit of good
kindling. Keep all your potato peelings, dry them in the
oven when baking and then store them in paper bags; they
can be used in place of kindling wood when lighting an
open fire. Just put a small bag of dry peelings in the hearth
and light one corner.

Cleaning Velcro

If Velcro fastenings on shoes or clothes become clogged with fluff they can be cleaned with a wire suede brush.

Efficient grilling

When grilling food, always line the grill pan with a layer of aluminium cooking foil. This saves energy by increasing the efficiency of the heat of the grill and also collects any dripped fat, thereby requiring less cleaning. After cooking leave the grill pan to cool until the fat solidifies, then simply roll it up and throw it in the bin.

Sticking plug

If you find that an electric plug is difficult to insert or remove from the socket then rub the metal prongs with a soft, graphite pencil and it should slide in and out much easier.

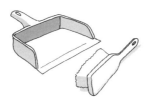

Brighter candles

To get candle wicks to burn much cleaner and brighter, soak the wicks in vinegar and allow to dry before lighting. A good tip is to always buy the best quality candles that you can. These will be made from paraffin wax and stearic acid, which helps the candle burn well, thus reducing dripping.

Wax removal

To easily remove melted candle wax from the candle holder – especially a glass one – place it in the freezer for one hour first. The wax should then easily and cleanly chip off.

Longer-lasting coal

If you have an open fire there is a very easy way to ensure that the coal you use burns brighter and lasts longer. Make up a solution of 2 tablespoons of washing soda (sodium carbonate) to 2 pints of water. Sprinkle this over the coal and let it dry before using on the fire. A handful of salt put onto a brightly burning fire at least once a week will reduce the build up of soot in the chimney.

Stuck playing cards

If playing cards are sticking together then rubbing the surface of them with a slice of white bread will make them easier to deal. Another way of getting rid of the stickiness is to brush the cards with talcum powder. This will absorb any sticky residues from greasy or sweaty fingers.

Red wine stain

Sponge a fresh red wine stain with white wine to keep it from setting or cover the area with salt and then soak in cold water. Spot treat with liquid detergent before washing as normal. Alternatively spray or pour a liberal amount of soda water onto the stain. This will dilute and neutralise the red wine. Leave the soda water soaking into the stain for 10 – 15 minutes then rinse it out and wash the garment or carpet as normal.

Tyre pressures

It is vital to always keep your vehicle tyre pressures at the correct levels. An easy way of remembering the pressures is to write them onto a small piece of masking tape and stick this to the rear of your tax disc holder on the windscreen. This will save time in finding the appropriate information at the garage forecourt or driving the vehicle with incorrect tyre pressures.

Stronger suction pads

To achieve much better strength on plastic suction pads, smear the pads with raw egg white before fixing to the wall.

Useful baby wipes

Baby wipes are a great way of cleaning many surfaces around the house as they remove dust and grime and disinfect at the same time. This makes them ideal for speedy bathroom cleaning jobs. They are especially useful if you find that guests are arriving unexpectedly and you don't have time to do a full dust and polish. A quick whip round with a few of baby wipes will do the trick!

Slippery Steps

In the frosty weather doorsteps can become slippery and dangerous. Washing the doorstep with a solution consisting of 1 soluble aspirin and 1 tbsp of methylated spirits to a bucket of water will prevent this from happening.

Freezer

If there is a power cut, remember not to open the freezer door. If left undisturbed, the food will remain frozen for up to 24 hours, but once the door has been opened the defrosting process will be greatly accelerated.

Slipping duvet

To help prevent a duvet from slipping off a child's bed, simply stitch a strip of material along the bottom of the duvet and tuck this under the mattress. This tip does not have to be limited to a child's duvet – we all tend to toss and turn a lot in bed!

Slipping grips

After a while, the rubber grips on bicycle handlebars can become loose and slide off. To prevent this from happening, paint that section of the handlebars with nail varnish remover and put the grips back on. They should stay in place.

Shoe polish stain

To remove shoe polish from clothing, try applying a waterless mechanic's soap or gel (available at DIY stores or car accessory shops). Rub this into the stain, leave for 30 minutes, then wash as usual. If any stain remains, try scrubbing with washing up liquid.

Rust-free rims

If the wheel rims of a bicycle have begun to go rusty the rust can be easily removed by placing pieces of emery paper between the bicycle brake blocks and turn the pedals whilst lightly applying the brakes.

Preserving pleats

To ensure that pleated skirts retain their perfect pleats after washing, hang them out to dry by the waistband with clothes pegs clipped to the bottom of the pleats to hold them in place.

Sweat stains

Sweat can be a very difficult stain to remove as it is made up of some of our body's most powerful pheromones and nature means it to stay put! Try one of these two methods… First sponge the stain with white wine vinegar, rinse and then wash on the hottest cycle safe for the particular material, using a biological washing powder or liquid. Alternatively crush three aspirins into a little warm water and make a paste with cream of tartar. Rub the paste into the sweat stain and leave to work for about 20 minutes before rinsing off and washing as normal.

Cleaning leather

Leather bags can be cleaned by rubbing them with the inside of a banana skin or, alternatively, with a cloth dipped in a little egg white that has been whisked until frothy. After cleaning, the leather should be polished with a soft cloth.

Soot stain

Never try rubbing to remove a soot stain from any fabric. Simply cover the area with salt and use a stiff brush.

Preserve children's art work

A quick coat of hairspray will stop any fading or smudging of the wonderful paintings that your children lovingly do for you!

Fresher carpets

A mixture of tea leaves and salt, sprinkled over a dull looking carpet then brushed or vacuumed off will restore and brighten the colours. Water from freshly boiled potatoes will also help to freshen a discoloured carpet as well as making it easier to remove mud stains. After using, rinse with clean water.

Clean windowsills

Spray exterior windowsills with furniture polish after washing to ensure that they stay clean longer, as dust and dirt will not stick to them so readily.

Clock cleaning

An ingenious way to clean the inside of a dusty clock without disturbing the mechanism is to place a ball of cotton wool soaked in paraffin in the base of the clock and leave for a few days. Dust from within the clock will be draw down onto the cotton wool leaving the internal workings clean.

Creased delicates

Delicate fabrics such as silk or velvet can be a nightmare to iron because of the added worry of scorching the fabric or making it shiny. Solve the problem by simply hanging these types of garments in a steamy bathroom. The creases will fall out with no ironing required.

Burnt pans

If a kitchen pan has burnt on food that seems impossible to shift then clean it by simmering some onion skins, in a little water, in it for an hour. Make sure that the pan does not boil dry during this time. Leave it to cool overnight and the blackened residues should easily clean off the following morning.

Barbeque pans

Cleaning the bottom of pans after use on the barbeque can be a messy job. If you remember to rub a bar of soap over the outside bottom of the pans before use then the black stains will wash off much easier.

Fresh microwave

To freshen up the inside of a microwave then simply put some lemon rind or a couple of tablespoons of lemon juice in the microwave and heat on full power for one minute.

Stuck stamps

If postage stamps have become stuck together, place them in the freezer for a short time. The intense cold freezes the layers of glue enabling you to cleave the stamps gently apart. You could say it's a 'first class' tip!

Wooden chopping board

A daily scrub with salt water will help restore discoloured wooden chopping or bread boards. Be sure to rub in the direction of the wood grain and finish off by rubbing the whole surface with a cut lemon to bleach it. Always try to dry a wooden chopping board outside as the sun's ultraviolet light will naturally disinfect the wood.

Roasting tins

Roasting tins should be periodically cleaned by soaking for an hour or so in a solution of biological washing powder and warm water. If there are any particularly bad stains then heating the solution on the hob for about ten minutes should help with their removal.

Drying duvet covers

Line drying of duvet covers and pillow cases can be speeded up by hanging them so that they form a 'bag' and attaching only one side of this to the line, so that air can enter and circulate inside.

Non-drip candles

Keep candles in the fridge for several hours before lighting
and you will find that they will drip a lot less.

Drying trousers

Trousers should be hung on the line by the ankle end. This effectively uses the weight of the waistband to minimise the creasing whilst the trousers are drying.

Laundry odours

Odours present in your laundry basket can be eliminated by placing a couple of fabric conditioner sheets at the bottom of the basket each week. One or two sheets can also be hung in a wardrobe to keep stored clothes smelling fresh. Used perfume or aftershave bottles also make great ways of masking odours by putting one at the bottom of the laundry basket, in your drawers or wardrobe.

Stored clothes

Clothes that are going into storage should not be given a final wash that contains fabric conditioner as this has been shown to accelerate mould growth on packed clothes.

Grubby trainers

Mud and grime on canvas shoes and trainers can
be cleaned off with carpet shampoo and an old, stiff
toothbrush. Once the worst of the dirt has been removed
most trainers respond perfectly well to a wash, on their
own, in the washing machine.

Towel care

New towels often shed fluff for the first couple of washes
so wash them on their own to avoid all your other
garments becoming covered. Remember that using fabric
conditioner when washing towels will gradually erode their
absorbency, so use it sparingly if at all.

Baseball caps

Trying to wash a baseball cap can easily destroy its
shape. If, however, you simply put it in the top rack of the
dishwasher and run on a hot cycle (with the dishes if you
like!), it will emerge clean and fresh ready to be hung by
the peak on the line to dry.

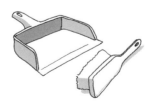

Flapping Shower Curtain

To prevent a shower curtain from flapping around sew either lead fishing weights or coins into a hem at the bottom. Do not use anything with iron content because the steam will cause rust which will stain the curtain fabric.

Pillow condition

Pillows will eventually reach the end of their natural, useable life. You can test to see if yours have reached this stage by placing the pillow horizontally across your forearm. If it droops badly at either end it is time to replace it. Pillows will also last longer if you protect them from the absorption of sweat, oils, perfumes and skin creams by using two pillow cases instead of one.

Shedding woollens

Spraying Angora sweaters and other fluffy woollen garments with a fine mist of hairspray will prevent them from shedding their fibres onto other clothes.

Curtain cleaning

Cleaning your own curtains at home can be a risky business as a lined curtain is made up of more than one type of fabric and each may respond to washing by shrinking at different rates. Even the threads of the hems etc. may shrink, causing puckered seams. If in any doubt don't take the risk – take the curtains to the dry cleaners instead.

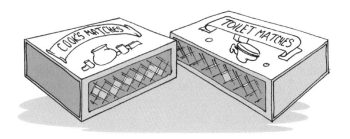

Bathroom odours

A quick way of masking an unpleasant odour in the bathroom is to light and extinguish a couple of matches. The aroma of the smoking match will linger and temporarily mask the smell. As a considerate host you should be ready to use this trick when you have guests who may use the bathroom in close succession – particularly following spicy food!

Lipstick stains

There are a few different things you can try to remove lipstick stains. On your best dining napkins, rub the stain gently with a little petroleum jelly or eucalyptus oil, taking care not to spread the stain. Then launder on a hot wash cycle with biological washing powder.

On other material or clothing sponging the lipstick with a mixture of baking soda and lemon juice then washing as normal should remove the stain completely.

Sticky labels

If you can't get an adhesive price label off something which you want to give as a gift, then simply popping it in the fridge for a while can often do the trick. This makes the label a lot easier to remove without leaving any sticky residue on the gift. If, however, you do end up with that annoying, sticky residue left by an adhesive label then this can be removed by either covering the area with a little talcum powder and then wiping with a dry cloth or using a little nail varnish remover on a piece of cotton wool.

Blood on clothing

Fresh bloodstains on clothes should be treated immediately by plunging the garment into cold, salted water for an hour. This helps to quickly dissolve the blood's albumen. Afterwards, wash with biological washing powder or liquid.

Water marks

If your water is leaving marks on your clothes this means that you are likely to have hard water. The hardness of water causes it to interfere with the effectiveness of detergent and leaves a film on the clothing. To remove this film, try soaking the clothes in a mixture of one gallon of water and one cup of vinegar. To prevent this from happening in the future, you can add a water conditioning product along with the detergent, or add a cup of borax. It will soften the water and freshen the wash as well.

Old facecloths

When a facecloth becomes very tatty or discoloured, cut off one corner and use it as a household cleaning cloth. (Cutting off the corner reminds you that it is not for faces!!)

Cool box for shopping

It is always useful to keep a picnic cool box in the car boot and use it for your frozen food when you have finished shopping. If you get stuck in traffic or need to make any unintended detours you don't need to panic about things thawing out.

Steamy mirrors

If you are fed up with the mirror steaming up whenever you run a bath or shower try one of these two solutions. When filling a bath run some cold water before the hot, to reduce the level of steam. Whenever you have to clean the bathroom mirror, use a small drop of washing up liquid on a paper towel to give the glass a final wipe over until it is free from smears. This fine coating of soap will keep the glass clear. The same can be achieved by rubbing the mirror with a little shaving foam then polishing off with a dry cloth.

Fine vacuum nozzle

If your vacuum cleaner nozzle just isn't fine enough for certain jobs then simply pop the cardboard tube from the inside of a kitchen paper roll over the end and cut or squash the other end as flat as you need it.

Dusting sock

A damp sock secured to the end of a broom handle with an elastic band is perfect for removing cobwebs in inaccessible places and is so much more effective than a feather duster. The dust and webbing sticks to the sock instead of falling on you!

Wooden floors

If you have a wooden floor that is looking a bit scratched and jaded then here is a great way of making it look good. Add a couple of tea bags to a bucket of warm water and wipe or mop the solution over the wood. This not only cleans the floor but the tea stain will also disguise any scratches and flaws!

Scratched glass

Remove scratches on glassware, watch glasses or mobile phone screens by polishing with toothpaste. The mild abrasives in the paste should blend the scratches away.

Scented pouches

If you are about to throw away old handkerchiefs, then think about recycling them into useful, scented pouches for clothes drawers, wardrobes and the airing cupboard. Simply place small sprigs of your favourite aromatic herbs and flowers, such as lavender and rosemary, in the centre of each handkerchief before tying the corners together with string or ribbon.

Free storage unit

The free cardboard wine carriers usually available from your local supermarket make great storage units for your household cleaning products. They are easy to carry around the house and keep everything neat and tidy under the sink or in the cupboard.

Cheap food covers

Shower caps freely available in many hotel bathrooms make really good food covers – and can be washed over and over again. They have an elastic rim which holds them perfectly in place over a plate or bowl and it saves on using cling film.

Perfect 'Thank-Yous'

At birthdays, Christmas etc. persuading the kids to write thank-you cards can be a nightmare! A fun way of solving this problem is to simply take a picture of your children holding up each of their presents as soon as they open them. You can then have prints made to use as thank-you postcards. If you have a digital camera the task is made even easier as you can quickly download the pictures and email them the same day.

Smelly food

Get into the habit of always putting meat bones and other smelly waste food into a scented nappy sack before it goes in the bin. This helps to deter unwelcome visits from foxes, cats, etc. to your bin bags. Even if you normally have no need for nappy sacks – buy some just for this tip!

That sickly stain!

Vomit! One of the most unpleasant stains to remove. If you have ever tried to remove it using normal cleaning solutions or bleach you have probably found that, in a few days, the unpleasant aroma soon returns! Here is the two stage process that you need to follow. Before even trying to remove the stain treat the area with white vinegar. This will neutralise the acids in the vomit and it will also drive away the smell. Then you can clean as normal to get rid of the actual stain and any germs.

Homemade wasp trap

A simple and effective wasp trap can be made by dropping a teaspoon of jam into a dilute solution of beer in a jar or glass. Cover the vessel with paper held in place with an elastic band, and poke a hole in the middle big enough for a wasp to enter. Wasps will be lured inside by the smell and quickly become intoxicated by the fumes. They will fall into the liquid and drown.

Washing labels

If you care for your clothes properly, they will almost certainly stay in better condition and thus last a lot longer.

General washing tips:

- Coloured garments last longer if they are washed inside out. This should ensure that any problems such as streaks on jeans, for example, can be avoided.

- Shirts retain their shape better if they are dried hanging on a clothes hanger. Straightening the seams and collar will make sure that the shape is better retained and the shirt then becomes easier to iron.

- Knitted garments always keep their shape better if they are dried flat.

- Never allow coloured garments to dry outdoors in sunlight. They can become discoloured and 'sun-bleached'.

Care label symbols

There are a number of symbols used internationally to give guidance as to the care of garments. These are in the following pages. If you encounter any that are not shown here then the best advice is to check with the manufacturer of the garment before attempting any cleaning.

Washing in water

The bowl symbol indicates that the garment can be washed in water in a washing machine or by hand. Within the bowl, there will either be a figure indicating the temperature, in degrees Celsius, that should be used to wash the garment or a series of dots representing temperature. The dots (for washing only) are interpreted as follows:

●   30°C (cool)

●●   40°C (warm)

●●●   50°C (hot)

●●
●●   60°C (very hot)

●●●
●●   70°C (extremely hot)

●●●
●●●   95°C (near boil)

The line under the bowl indicates any limitations to the normal washing process.

Wash in a filled machine at the indicated water temperature. Use normal spin.

Wash in a machine at the indicated water temperature. The machine should only be half filled. Spin for one minute only. In a separate spin dryer, spin for half a minute only. The line under the bowl indicates that extra care should be taken.

The above sets of washing instructions may also be seen represented as follows:

Wash in a domestic or commercial machine in water not exceeding 30°C, at normal setting.

Wash in a domestic or commercial machine in water not exceeding 30°C, at permanent press setting.

Wash in a domestic or commercial machine in water not exceeding 30°C, at delicate/gentle setting.

Wash in a domestic or commercial machine in water not exceeding 40°C, at normal setting.

Wash in a domestic or commercial machine in water not exceeding 40°C, at permanent press setting.

Wash in a domestic or commercial machine in water not exceeding 40°C, at delicate/gentle setting.

Wash in a domestic or commercial machine in water not exceeding 50°C, at normal setting.

 Wash in a domestic or commercial machine in water not exceeding 50°C, at permanent press setting.

 Wash in a domestic or commercial machine in water not exceeding 50°C, at delicate/gentle setting.

 Wash in a domestic or commercial machine in water not exceeding 60°C, at normal setting.

 Wash in a domestic or commercial machine in water not exceeding 60°C, at permanent press setting.

 Wash in a domestic or commercial machine in water not exceeding 70°C, at normal setting.

 Wash in a domestic or commercial machine in water not exceeding 70°C, at permanent press setting.

 Wash in a commercial machine in water not exceeding 95°C, at normal setting.

 Wash in a commercial machine in water not exceeding 95°C, at permanent press setting.

 Wash in a domestic or commercial machine at any temperature, at normal setting.

Hand washing

Always make sure that the washing powder is completely dissolved in the water before immersing the garment. Never sprinkle or pour washing powder directly onto the garment or allow coloured garments to soak. This can result in discolouration.

 Hand wash only. Max. 40°C. Do not rub and do not ring out.

 Do not wash in water.

 Wash gently by hand in water not exceeding 30°C.

 Wash gently by hand in water not exceeding 40°C.

Washing of wool and silk garments

Garments of untreated wool or silk, for example, with washing instructions "hand wash, max 40°C", demand special care. Use a washing powder that is specifically intended for 40°C washing in water. Do not soak. Wash directly in water of the correct temperature with the washing powder well dissolved in the water. Gently squeeze the garment in the washing water but do not rub or ring out. Rinse thoroughly in clean water of the same temperature. A short spin is the best way of removing excess water. Shake out the garment once it is half dry, to give it a "fuller" feel. Dry heavy knitted garments by laying them flat.

Ironing

The iron symbol means that the garment can be normally ironed or a rotary iron used. Within the symbol there are a number of dots to indicate the ironing temperature.

 High temperature, with or without steam by hand or press on commercial equipment. Max.200°C. For example cotton or linen items.

 Medium temperature, with or without steam by hand or press on commercial equipment. Max.150°C. For example polyester, rayon, triacetate and wool or natural silk textiles.

 Low temperature, max.110°C. For example polyamide, acrylic, modacrylic, acetate, nylon, polypropylene and spandex textiles.

 Do not iron using steam

Chlorine bleaching

The triangle represents bleaching instructions for that the garment.

 Can be bleached with any bleach when required.

 Can be bleached with chlorine.

 Use only non-chlorine bleach when required.

 Must not be bleached.

Dry Cleaning

The circle indicates that the garment can be dry cleaned.
The letter inside the circle indicates the type of dry cleaning
fluid to be used.

 Will not stand a dry cleaning fluid, such
as trichloroethylene, that is stronger than
perchloroethane (the most common dry cleaning
fluid used).

 Dry cleaning fluid such as perchloroethane. The
limitation indicated by the line beneath refers to
the water added, the mechanical process used
and/or the drying temperature.

 Will not stand a dry cleaning fluid that is stronger
than naphtha.

 Do not dry clean.

Drying

The rectangle is a symbol for drying. Water must removed from the textile before drying. Virtually all textiles can be given a short spin, for a maximum of one minute. Many garments can also be tumble dried. Garments with a Gore-Tex membrane should, for example, be tumble dried for best results. On the other hand, avoid tumble drying garments that you particularly cherish, as regular tumble drying will gradually wear the garment. The most important thing is to follow the symbol that indicates whether or not the garment should be tumble dried.

 Any heat

 Do not tumble dry

 No heat / air dry

 Low heat (not exceeding 55°C) on normal setting.

 Low heat (not exceeding 55°C) on permanent press setting.

 Low heat (not exceeding 55°C) on delicate cycle.

 Medium heat (not exceeding 65°C) on normal setting.

 Medium heat (not exceeding 65°C) on permanent press setting.

 High heat (not exceeding 75°C) on normal setting.

After extraction of excess water, line dry or hang to dry.

Hang up the soaking wet article to "drip" dry.

 After extraction of excess water, dry the article on a suitable flat surface.

 Dry in the shade (usually accompanies a line dry, drip dry, or dry flat symbol).

Supplementary care symbols

Do not wring garment to remove water.

Can be wet-cleaned. (A new professional 'solvent-free' service).

Must not be wet-cleaned. (A new professional 'solvent-free' service).

Conversion charts

Weight & measure conversions

Length:

1 millimetre (mm)		= 0.0394 inch (in)
1 centimetre (cm)	= 10 mm	= 0.0394 in
1 metre (m)	= 100 cm	= 1.0936 yard (yd)
1 kilometre (km)	= 1,000 m	= 0.6214 mile

1 inch		= 2.54 cm
1 foot (ft)	= 12 in	= 0.3048 m
1 yard	= 3 ft	= 0.9144 m
1 mile	= 1,760 yd	= 1.6093 km

Area:

1 square cm (cm²)	= 100 mm²	= 0.1550 in²
1 square m (m²)	= 10,000 cm²	= 1.1960 yd²
1 square km (km²)	= 100 hectares	= 0.3861 mile²

1 square in (in²)		= 6.4516 cm²
1 square ft (ft²)	= 144 in²	= 0.0929 m²
1 square yd (yd²)	= 9 ft²	= 0.8361 m²
1 acre	= 4,840 yd²	= 4,046.9 m²
1 square mile (mile²)	= 640 acres	= 2.590 km²

Volume:

1 cubic cm (cm³)		= 0.0610 in³
1 cubic decimetre (dm³)	= 1,000 cm³	= 0.0353 ft³
1 cubic m (m³)	= 1,000 dm³	= 1.3080 yd³
1 litre (l)	= 1 dm³	
	= 1000 millilitre (ml)	= 1.76 pint (pt)
	= 2.113 US pt	
1 hectolitre (hl)	= 100 l	= 21.997 gallon (gal)
		= 26.417 US gal

1 cubic in (in³)		= 16.387 cm³
1 cubic ft (ft³)	= 1,728 in³	= 0.0283 m³
1 cubic yd (yd³)	– 27 ft³	= 0.7646 m³
1 fluid ounce (fl oz)		= 28.413 ml
1 pint (pt)	= 20 fl oz	= 0.5683 l
1 gallon (gal)	= 8 pt	= 4.546 l
		= 1.201 US gal

Mass:

1 milligram (mg)		= 0.0154 grain
1 gram (g)	= 1,000 mg	= 0.0353 ounce (oz)
1 metric carat	= 0.2 g	= 3.0865 grains
1 kilogram (kg)	= 1,000 g	= 2.2046 pound (lb)
1 tonne (t)	= 1,000 kg	= 0.9842 ton

1 oz	= 437.5 grains	= 28.35 g
1 lb	= 16 oz	= 0.4536 kg
1 stone	= 14 lb	= 6.3503 kg
1 hundredweight (cwt)	= 112 lb	= 50.802 kg
1 ton	= 20 cwt	= 1.016 t

Temperature conversions

Celsius °C	Fahrenheit °F	Celsius °C	Fahrenheit °F
-30°C	-22°F	16°C	60.8°F
-20°C	-4.0°F	17°C	62.6°F
-10°C	14.0°F	18°C	64.4°F
0°C	32.0°F	19°C	66.2°F
1°C	33.8°F	20°C	68.0°F
2°C	35.6°F	21°C	69.8°F
3°C	37.4°F	22°C	71.6°F
4°C	39.2°F	23°C	73.4°F
5°C	41.0°F	24°C	75.2°F
6°C	42.8°F	25°C	77.0°F
7°C	44.6°F	26°C	78.8°F
8°C	46.4°F	27°C	80.6°F
9°C	48.2°F	28°C	82.4°F
10°C	50.0°F	29°C	84.2°F
11°C	51.8°F	30°C	86.0°F
12°C	53.6°F	40°C	104°F
13°C	55.4°F	50°C	122°F
14°C	57.2°F	60°C	140°F
15°C	59.0°F		

To convert Fahrenheit to Centigrade: $C = 5/9 \times (F-32)$

To convert Centigrade to Fahrenheit: $F = (9/5 \times C) + 32$

Index

Index

Index

Index

Notes

Notes

'The Greatest Tips in the World' series . . .

Also available:

ISBN 1-905151-03-9
Pub Date: Sept 2005

ISBN 1-905151-01-1
Pub Date: April 2006

ISBN 1-905151-04-7
Pub Date: Sept 2005

ISBN 1-905151-05-5
Pub Date: Sept 2005

ISBN 1-905151-06-3
Pub Date: Oct 2004

ISBN 1-905151-09-8
Pub Date: April 2006

ISBN 1-905151-08-X
Pub Date: April 2006

ISBN 1-905151-07-1
Pub Date: April 2006

ISBN 1-905151-11-X
Pub Date: Sept 2006

ISBN 1-905151-12-8
Pub Date: Sept 2006

ISBN 1-905151-13-6
Pub Date: Sept 2006

With many more to follow, these books will form a most useful compilation for any bookshelf.

Other 'The Greatest in the World' products . . .

DVDs

'The Greatest Gardening Tips in the World' - presented by Steve Brookes
(release date: September 2005)

'The Greatest Cat Tips in the World' - presented by Joe Inglis
(release date: September 2006)

'The Greatest Dog Tips in the World' - presented by Joe Inglis
(release date: September 2006)

'The Greatest Golfing Tips in the World' - Vols. 1 & 2 - presented by
John Cook (release date: September 2006)

'The Greatest Yoga Tips in the World' - presented by David Gellineau and
David Robson (release date: September 2005)

'The Greatest Cat Cuisine in the World' - presented by Joe Inglis
(release date: September 2006)

'The Greatest Dog Cusine in the World' - presented by Joe Inglis
(release date: September 2006)

Hardback, full-colour books:

'The Greatest Cat Cuisine in the World' - by Joe Inglis
ISBN 1-905151-14-4 (publication date: September 2006)

'The Greatest Dog Cuisine in the World' - by Joe Inglis
ISBN 1-905151-15-2 (publication date: September 2006)

For more information about currently available and forthcoming book and
DVD titles please visit:

www.thegreatestintheworld.com

or write to:
Public Eye Publications
PO Box 3182
Stratford-upon-Avon
Warwickshire CV37 7XW
United Kingdom

Tel / Fax: +44(0)1789 299616
Email: info@publiceyepublications.co.uk

The Author

Vicky Burford is a busy young mother who manages to balance the demands of a young family whilst keeping her sanity and a relatively well-organised household! Vicky stays at home to look after her four young children, all under the age of 9 years. Prior to this Vicky worked in London as a PA. She is also the author of another book in the series - 'The Greatest Baby & Toddler Tips in the World'.